Spiritual Basics
Workbook

A Guide for New Believers

by David Rhoades

Table of Contents

Preface

"To all who received Jesus, who believed in his name, he gave the right to become children of God" (John 1:12).[1] If you believe in the Lord Jesus Christ, you are an adopted child of God. Welcome to God's family!

Just as God has designed children to grow, he has designed you to grow spiritually. *Spiritual Basics: A Guide for New Believers* is a guide that can help. This guide is designed for self-study, but you will get the greatest benefit if you work through it with the help of another Christian or a small group of believers.

This guide will always be completely free at faithcoach.org. Download, print and share copies as you need.

Gratitude and Permissions

Spiritual Basics is an adaptation of George Patterson's "Seven Basic Commands of Christ." Patterson was a missionary who developed an effective way of helping new believers continue their journey of faith and help their friends do the same. I am grateful for his service to the Lord.

It is my desire that God uses *Spiritual Basics* for the greatest benefit to his Kingdom.

- You may distribute this workbook to others on the condition that you give it to them for free. "Freely you have received, freely give."

- You may translate this workbook into other languages.

- You may make changes in the content of this workbook so that it better fits your context.

Getting Started

God has made a promise to people who believe in Christ: "I will never leave you nor forsake you" (Hebrew 13:5).

If you are a new believer, make sure you meet regularly with some other maturing believers. They are a part of your spiritual family. They will pray with you and help you as you deal with life's issues.

---

[1] Unless otherwise noted, Scripture quotations are from The Holy Bible, English Standard Version® (ESV®), copyright © 2001 by Crossway, a publishing ministry of Good News Publishers. Used by permission. All rights reserved.

My prayer for you is that you will begin to discover the apostle Paul's appeal to the Christians at Rome in the first century A.D.: *"Present your bodies as a living sacrifice, holy and acceptable to God, which is your spiritual worship. Do not be conformed to this world, but be transformed by the renewal of your mind, that by testing you may discern what is the will of God, what is good and acceptable and perfect"* (Romans 12:1-2).

In Christ,

Dr. David H. Rhoades

Additional resources may be available at faithcoach.org. For any assistance or questions, contact me at david@davidrhoades.org.

Introduction

Our Bible Study Method

As a new believer in the Lord Jesus Christ, you need to understand the importance of the Bible in your life. The Bible is God's Word. As you read or hear the Bible, God will continue to transform your life into the image of his Son.

Hebrews 4:12 says, *"For the word of God is living and active, sharper than any two-edged sword, piercing to the division of soul and of spirit, of joints and of marrow, and discerning the thoughts and intentions of the heart."*

This illustration of a sword can help us understand any passage of the Bible.

1. The arrow that points up is for God. **What do I learn about God?**

2. The handle is for man. **What do I learn about man?**

3. The blade that cuts one direction asks, **Is there an example to follow?**

4. The blade that cuts the other direction asks, **Is there a command to obey?**

After reading or hearing any story from the Bible, ask these four questions one at a time and search the story for answers. The answers you find can reveal how the story might apply to your life.

In this workbook, we will discover seven important commands Jesus gave all of his followers. You may want to explore one command each day for the next seven days. Seek out a pastor or trusted believer if you have additional questions.

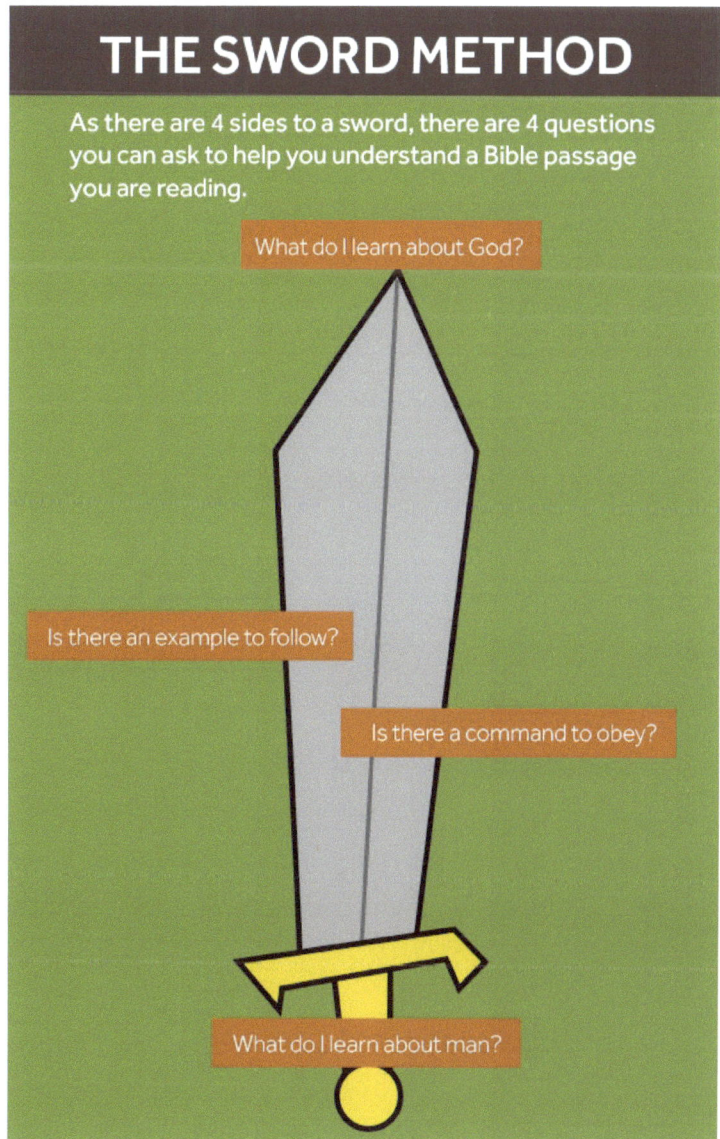

THE SWORD METHOD

As there are 4 sides to a sword, there are 4 questions you can ask to help you understand a Bible passage you are reading.

What do I learn about God?

Is there an example to follow?

Is there a command to obey?

What do I learn about man?

Command #1 — Repent and Believe

The Command

Find the following verse in your Bible and write out what Jesus said:

Mark 1:15 - _____

_____

_____

A Story About Repenting and Believing

Read the story the encounter between Zacchaeus and Jesus. It is found in **Luke 19:1-10**.

What did you learn about God? _____

_____

_____

What did you learn about man? _____

_____

_____

Is there an example to follow? _____

_____

_____

Is there a command to obey? _____

_____

_____

What Does "Repent" Mean?

Repent means to turn from sin and follow Jesus.

What Does "Believe" Mean?

Believe means to choose to trust Jesus as your Lord.

Why Should We Repent and Believe?

Write your answers based on what these verses teach:

Romans 3:23 - _____

_____

Romans 6:23 - _____

_____

Romans 10:9-10 - _____

_____

Who Should Repent?

Read Acts 2:38-41. The only way to be forgiven for sin is to repent. Therefore **everyone should repent.**

What Is Assurance?

Read 1 John 1:9. This verse teaches that when we confess our sins Jesus forgives us and cleanses us.

Read John 10:28. We can have assurance that we are saved from our sins because we are secure in Jesus.

Prayer

"Jesus, confess that I have sinned against you. I want to leave my old life of sin and follow you. I believe in you. You are my Lord, and I will obey you."

Assignment

Tell someone about your decision to follow Jesus. Perhaps you know of someone who has been praying for you. Or maybe there is someone who invited you to follow Jesus, but you were not yet ready. Or perhaps you would like to tell your best friend or closest family member. It is important that we follow Jesus openly, for he said, "Everyone who acknowledges me before men, I also will acknowledge before my Father who is in heaven" (Matthew 10:32).

Command #2 — Be Baptized

The Command

Find the following verse in your Bible and write out what Jesus said:

Matthew 28:19 - _____

_____

_____

A Story About Baptism

Read the story the encounter between Philip and a new believer. It is found in **Acts 8:26-39**.

What did you learn about God? _____

_____

_____

What did you learn about man? _____

_____

_____

Is there an example to follow? _____

_____

_____

Is there a command to obey? _____

_____

_____

·

What Is Baptism?

Baptism is the public identification of your life with Jesus Christ. When a person is baptized, he or she is gently submerged under and raised out of the water.

Who Should Be Baptized?

Water baptism is intended only for the person who has believed in the good news about Jesus Christ and become His disciple (follower).

Why Should I Be Baptized?

1. **To obey the command of Christ.**

   Jesus said to his disciples, *"Go, therefore, and make disciples of all people, <u>baptizing</u> them in the name of the Father and of the Son and of the Holy Spirit"* (Matt. 28:19).

2. **To show others that you are a disciple of Christ.**

   Baptism is a public testimony that you are following Jesus now. You identify with him. Just as Jesus died, was buried, and was resurrected from the grave, baptism shows that you identify with him. You have died to an old way of living, buried it, and now you are raised to live a new life.

3. **To follow the example of Christ.**

   When Jesus began his ministry, he was baptized by John the Baptist. The life Jesus lived is an example of how we should live.

When Should I Be Baptized?

As soon as you have believed in the good news about Jesus Christ! In the New Testament, baptisms are never delayed.

How Should I Be Baptized?

By immersion!

- The word "baptize" in Greek (the original language of the New Testament) literally means to plunge, submerge or immerse.

- Our union with Christ's death and resurrection is best expressed through immersion.

- The baptisms in the New Testament were by immersion.

Where Should I Be Baptized?

Wherever there is water!

Prayer

"Lord, give me the strength to identify my life with you by being baptized."

Assignment

If you have not yet been baptized, please speak to a pastor or trusted believer about your desire to be baptized. They should be able to answer any additional questions you have and help you be baptized.

Command #3 — Pray

The Command

What phrase does **Matthew 6:5** begin with? _____

Notice that the same phrase is found in each of the next two verses.

A Story About Prayer

Read what Jesus said about prayer in **Matthew 6:5-15**.

What did you learn about God? _____

_____

_____

What did you learn about man? _____

_____

_____

Is there an example to follow? _____

_____

_____

Is there a command to obey? _____

_____

_____

What Is Prayer?

Prayer is talking with God our Father.

Why Do We Pray?

God hears us when we pray. Also, prayer expresses our desire for God's will to be accomplished on earth.

Are there other reasons you can think of why we should pray? If so, what?

_____

_____

_____

_____

How Do We Pray?

We pray simply by talking with God.

"Give us this day our daily bread" — We pray for our needs.

"Forgive us our debts" — We pray for daily cleansing of sin.

"Deliver us from evil" — We pray for resistance from temptation.

What other ways can you make the prayer of **Matthew 6:9-13** personalized?

_____

_____

_____

_____

Prayer

"Lord, teach me to pray. Give me pure motives when I pray. May your will be done in my life."

Assignment

Start and finish today and tomorrow by giving thanks to God and presenting your requests to Him. Try to make praying each morning and night a daily habit. You can pray any time of the day in any situation. God is always there.

Command #4 — Go and Make Disciples

The Command

Read what Jesus told his disciples in **Matthew 28:19-20**.

A Story About Sharing Jesus with Others

Read the encounter between the Samaritan woman and Jesus. It is found in **John 4:4-42**.

What did you learn about God? _____

_____

_____

What did you learn about man? _____

_____

_____

Is there an example to follow? _____

_____

_____

Is there a command to obey? _____

_____

_____

Who Should We Share Jesus With?

Read John 4:16. We share Jesus with our families, friends, and neighbors.

What Should We Say?

Read John 4:29. The woman shared her story about her encounter with Jesus.

Write down how you met Jesus: _____

_____

_____

_____

_____

_____

_____

Who Is Qualified To Go?

In John 4, the Samaritan woman was qualified. **Every believer is qualified to go**.

Prayer

"Lord, make me bold to share what you have done in my life. Give me your words to share with others I know."

Assignment #1: Your Story

Write out your story with three parts:

Your life before Jesus:_____

_____

_____

_____

_____

_____

How you met Jesus: _____

_____

_____

_____

_____

_____

_____

Your life since meeting Jesus: _____

_____

_____

_____

_____

_____

Assignment #2: God's Story

Practice sharing the good news of Jesus by drawing out this bridge illustration featuring Romans 6:23:[2]

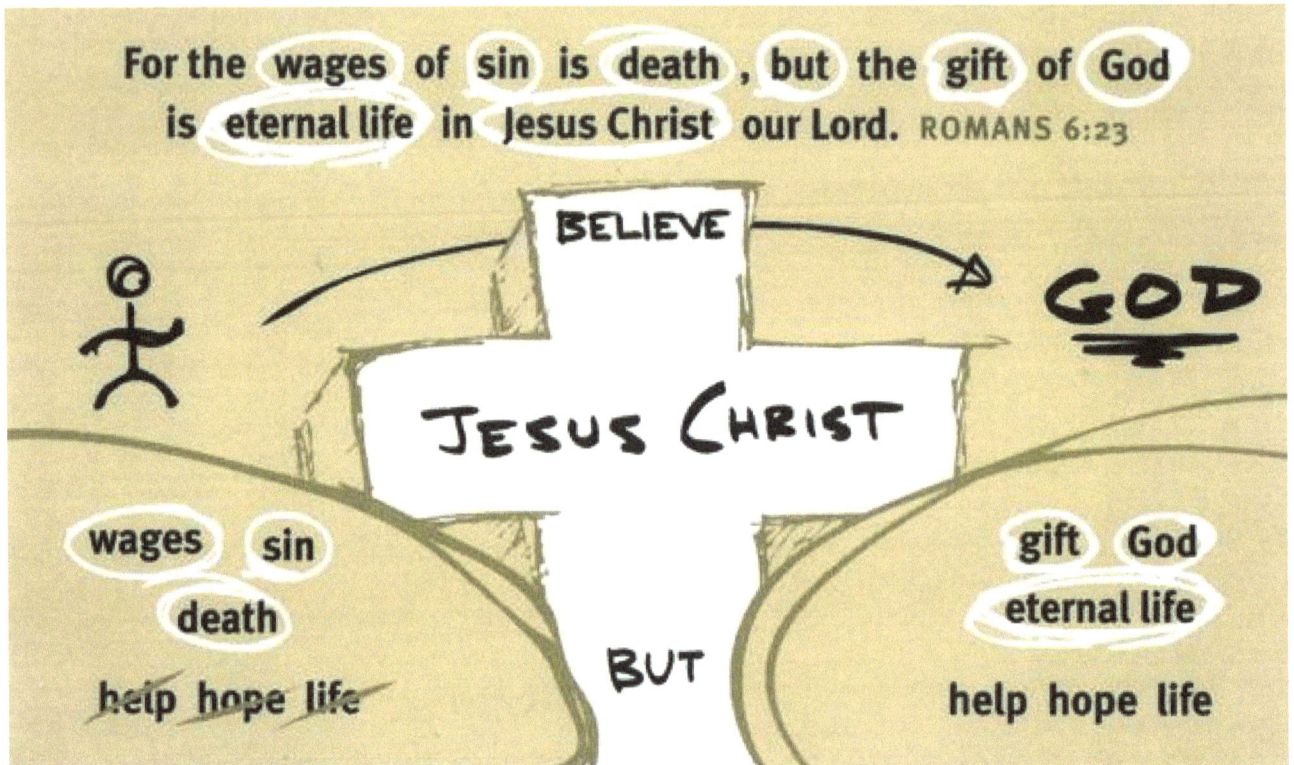

---

[2] Used by permission from NavPress, all rights reserved. ONE VERSE EVANGELISM, © 2000 by Randy Raysbook. http://www.navpress.com/product/9780972902366/One-Verse-Evangelism-Randy-Raysbrook-and-Steve-Walker

Command #5 — Love

The Command

Find **Matthew 22:37-39** in your Bible and write out the two types of persons we are to love:

    The Greatest Command: Love _____.

    The 2nd-Greatest Command: Love _____.

A Story About Love

Read the parable of the Good Samaritan. It is found in **Luke 10:25-37**.

    What did you learn about God? _____

_____

_____

    What did you learn about man? _____

_____

_____

    Is there an example to follow? _____

_____

_____

    Is there a command to obey? _____

_____

_____

What Is Love?

Write your thoughts about these Scriptures:

John 15:13 - _____

_____

_____

_____

1 Corinthians 13 - _____

_____

_____

_____

Why Do We Love?

Read John 13:34-35. We love because Jesus loved us first. Love also teaches the world about Jesus.

Who Do We Love?

According to **Matthew 22:37-39**, our first priority must be to love God. Then we need to love our neighbor.

How Do We Love?

Read John 14:15. Loving Jesus means we obey Jesus.

Read John 21:17. Loving others means telling them what God has done for you.

Prayer

"Lord, help me to love you by obeying you. Lord, help me to love others so they might learn that you love them."

Assignment

What is a tangible way to show love to someone you may encounter today? Do it!

Command #6 — Receive the Lord's Supper

The Command

Find **Luke 22:19-20** in your Bible and write out what the two items of the Lord's Supper symbolize:

The bread stands for _____.

The cup stands for _____.

A Story About the Lord's Supper

Read the story of how Jesus started the Lord's Supper. It is found in **Luke 22:7-20**.

What did you learn about God? _____

_____

_____

What did you learn about man? _____

_____

_____

Is there an example to follow? _____

_____

_____

Is there a command to obey? _____

_____

_____

What Is the Lord's Supper?

Read 1 Corinthians 11:26. The Lord's Supper is an action that symbolized the Lord's death.

Why Do We Receive the Lord's Supper?

Read 1 Corinthians 11:26. We receive the Lord's Supper because Jesus' body was broken for us and His blood was spilled for us.

How Do We Receive the Lord's Supper?

Read 1 Corinthians 11:27-29. We must examine ourselves, confess our sins to God and remember Jesus died to give us forgiveness.

Who Should Receive the Lord's Supper?

Read Acts 2:42 and 1 Corinthians 11:27-29. The Lord's Supper should be received by baptized, devoted disciples of Jesus who examine themselves.

Prayer

"Lord, show me the sins I have committed. Cleanse me of them. Thank you for your forgiveness. Thank you for giving your body and blood for me."

Assignment

Receive the Lord's Supper with your church the next time it is offered. It is good to gather with God's family whenever possible. As a member of God's family, you will be encouraged by others and others will encourage you.

Session 7 — Give

The Command

Find **Luke 6:38** in your Bible and write out the promise made to those who give:

When I give, what will happen?_____

_____

A Story About Giving

Read the story of the giving widow. It is found in **Mark 12:41-44**.

What did you learn about God? _____

_____

_____

What did you learn about man? _____

_____

_____

Is there an example to follow? _____

_____

_____

Is there a command to obey? _____

_____

_____

What Should We Give to God?

Our money, our time and our lives.

Why Should We Give to God?

Read 1 Corinthians 9:6-7. If we give generously, we will receive generously. God loves a cheerful giver.

How Do We Give to God?

Read 2 Corinthians 9:7. We should give cheerfully, not under compulsion or guilt.

Read Matthew 6:1-4. We should give secretly, not for recognition.

Who Do We Give To?

Read 2 Corinthians 9. A collection was given to a church.

Read 1 Timothy 5:17, Romans 15:24, and Acts 4:34-35. The church is to finance its mandate to share the good news of Jesus, provide financial support of its pastors, and give to those who have needs.

Prayer

"Lord, everything I have is yours. Teach me to give. Show me needs that I can help with my time and money."

Assignment

Decide this week an amount of time or money you will give for the work of the church each week. If you have a family, discuss this with them.

What's Next?

Your journey with God has just begun!

Here are a few practices that will help you grow in Christ for the rest of your life:

Pray to God every day.

Prayer is communicating with God. He wants to be your closest friend and greatest help. Whatever is going on in your life, tell him about it. You won't be telling God something he doesn't already know—God knows everything! But the more you talk with him, the closer you become to him. And drawing close to God will change your heart for the better.

Read your Bible every day.

There are many things in this world to fill your mind, many of which are harmful to your spiritual health. But the Bible is a resource like no other. It is the very Word of God. It is his message to us—the story of his love for us. You are transformed into the image of Jesus Christ as you put God's Word in your heart.

Gather with God's people (the church) on a regular basis.

It is best if you can join together with other followers of Christ on a weekly basis (or even more often). Remember, no one is perfect and no church is perfect. But you will find some believers who will be especially encouraging as you continue your spiritual journey.

A Final Word

If I can help you with any questions, you may contact me at david@davidrhoades.org. Also, you will find additional resources for your Christian journey at faithcoach.org. You can read my blog and learn from my teaching ministry at davidrhoades.org.

In Christ,

Dr. David H. Rhoades